AFFIRM

When God Stamps His Approval

Eve "Starr" Geiggar

AFFIRM
When God Stamps His Approval

Copyright © 2025, Eve "Starr" Geiggar
Contact the Author via e-mail at
MadeToManifest2022@gmail.com.

All rights reserved. No part of this book may be reproduced, stored in a retrieved system, or transmitted in any form or any means, electronic, mechanical, photocopying, recording, scanning, or otherwise, without the prior written permission of the author.

Authors: Eve "Starr" Geiggar
Publication Services: Kingdom News Today

DISCLAIMER
All the material contained in this book is provided for educational and informational purposes only. No responsibility can be taken for any results or outcomes resulting from the use of this material.

While every attempt has been made to provide information that is both accurate and effective, the author does not assume any responsibility for the accuracy or use/misuse of this information.

Printed in the United States of America.
ISBN 978-1-955127-40-0

Introduction

"As Far as I Can Remember..."

As far as I can remember, I've lived a life of fear, afraid to move, scared to be, and afraid to do, trapped in a world of rigidity, anxiety, and negative thoughts. Yet deep down, a whisper kept reminding me: *This is not the way.* That whisper was the voice of God.

And in a dream, He gave me a word. One word. One cover. One title: *Affirm.*

Affirm means to declare that something is true. To support with strength. To validate and confirm.

But this book isn't about the world's validation, but God's affirmation.

When God affirms you, no one can revoke it. When God rewrites your story, no one can edit it. This book is a journey through being affirmed by the One who never changes, even when everything around us does.

Affirm

Definition of Affirm

Affirm (verb)
- To state as a fact, assert strongly and publicly
- To offer emotional support or encouragement
- To declare one's truth and identity

Spiritual Definition
- When God declares you chosen, equipped, and set apart according to His will and purpose

Scripture Foundation
- *"Now it is God who makes both us and you stand firm in Christ. He anointed us, set his seal of ownership on us, and put his Spirit in our hearts as a deposit, guaranteeing what is to come."* — 2 Corinthians 1:21-22 (KJV)

Table of Contents

Chapter 1: Scared to Move, Scared to Be ....

Chapter 2: Overcoming War Within..................

Chapter 3: When God Speaks ....

Chapter 4: From Barren to Fruitful ....

Chapter 5: Approved by God—Now What? .....

Chapter 6: Breaking the Cycle ....

Chapter 7: Faith That Overrides Fear ....

Chapter 8: Change in Order to Become ....

Chapter 9: When Enough Is Enough.................

Chapter 10: Now That You Know.....................

Conclusion: The Becoming Continues ....

Closing Prayer ....

Chapter 1
Scared to Move, Scared to Be

Theme: Living in Fear, Feeling Stuck

Scripture: *"For God has not given us the spirit of fear, but of power, love, and a sound mind."* – 2 Timothy 1:7 (KJV)

Prayer: Lord, I confess the fear that has gripped me for too long. But today, I chose courage. I step out of the shadows and into Your light. Empower me to move forward. Amen.

When God Stamps His Approval

The Fear I Carried

As far back as I can remember, fear was there, not just fear of things but of everything. Fear of living, fear of dying, fear of being seen, and fear of being unseen. Fear of failure, fear of success, fear of not knowing what to do, fear of doing the wrong thing, fear of being too much, and fear of not being enough.

Yet, somehow, I still showed up. I smiled. I functioned. I achieved. But underneath that was a life drenched in dread and soaked in survival.

I used to think it all started in 2020, when COVID changed everything. But truthfully, fear had always been there, waiting quietly in the background of my choices. I just hadn't stopped long enough to confront it.

But when I decided to walk differently, to choose God's way over the world's way, I should've known the enemy would try to shake me. And he did. His weapon of choice? Fear.

Even though I was raised in the Word and read 2 Timothy 1:7 repeatedly, even though I knew what God said about fear, I still let it

AFFIRM

live rent-free in my mind, heart, and decisions.

I believed God's Word but hadn't applied it to my identity. I hadn't declared it loud enough to break the chains.

Living Rigid, Loving Fear

I lived in fear for so long that it became normal. Fear was my comfort zone, and freedom felt foreign.

Something felt wrong if I wasn't afraid, as if peace was too suspicious to trust. I lived in a rigid place, where movement felt like punishment and stillness felt like shame.

And no matter how many promises God made to me… No matter how often I read that I am fearfully and wonderfully made… No matter how often I heard I was the righteousness of God… I still let fear settle in.

I knew better, but I didn't *do* better because fear can disguise itself as wisdom, caution, and logic. But make no mistakes, fear is a liar. And I was done living by lies.

When God Stamps His Approval

When I Finally Said No to Fear

One day, I decided. Fear is not my future. Fear is not my identity. Fear is not my portion.

Fear is not from God. I began to speak back. To affirm what *God* said about me. To silence the inner critic with the louder voice of truth. I found my weapon in His Word. I found my strength in His Spirit. And one verse rang loudly in my heart: *"Perfect love casts out fear."* (1 John 4:18) But what is perfect love? I asked myself. I turned to Corinthians 13 where it says, *"Love is patient, kind, and does not envy or boast. It keeps no record of wrongs. It always hopes, protects, and perseveres."* God is perfect love. And then came a revelation: I wasn't walking in perfect love because I didn't love *myself.*

The Layers Beneath the Fear

Fear was the surface emotion. But under fear was shame. Under shame was rejection. Under rejection was abandonment. And beneath it all… was a whisper. A still, small voice. The voice of God. The voice saying, *"I am with you. I called you. I never left you."*

AFFIRM

Even when fear shouted, God whispered. And His whisper has the power to silence every scream.

Chapter 2
Overcoming War Within

Theme: Overcoming Fear, Internal Battles, and Self-Doubt

Scripture: *"For I know the plans I have for you," declares the Lord, "plans to prosper you and not to harm you, plans to give you a hope and a future."*—Jeremiah 29:11 (NIV)

Prayer: Lord, today I declare that I am an overcomer. Though fear has gripped me, You have freed me. I thank You for Your thoughts toward me—thoughts of peace, purpose, and power. Let Your truth rise above every lie I've believed about myself. In You, I live boldly. Amen.

AFFIRM

When God Affirms, But Fear Still Speaks

Fear didn't just make me anxious; it made me stuck. It wasn't just a passing thought; it became a stronghold. Even when God called me chosen... Even when He whispered promises in my ear... Even when I stood on stages or sat in silence, I knew He had affirmed me... Fear still found a way to talk me out of believing it. That's what fear does. It *distracts* you. It *destroys* your confidence. It *delays* your purpose. It *disguises* itself as caution, humility, even "wisdom." And it will do whatever it takes to keep you bound, in the same place, thinking the same thoughts, praying the same prayers, with no movement.

How Can I Be Free and Still Feel Bound?

My question was: *How can I be free and still feel bound?* I've read the scriptures. I've spoken the promises. I've worshipped, I've served, I've prayed... But I still struggled to move forward in who God said I was. I had to face it: I wasn't just afraid; I had allowed fear to define me. It became my internal identity, not just an emotion. But even in that, God kept affirming me. He kept blessing me. He kept showing up, because He never changes His mind about me.

When God Stamps His Approval

Overcoming: A Daily Decision

This chapter isn't about one moment of breakthrough—it's about a lifestyle of overcoming. You overcome by your actions:
- Daily, I put on the whole armor.
- Daily, I decide to believe the truth over feelings.
- Daily, I remind myself that fear is not my portion.
- Daily, I remember what fear cost me… and what freedom has restored.

Fear robbed me, but I also allowed it. I allowed it to steal my voice, delay my obedience, and block my blessings. But I don't live there anymore. I rise because God has already affirmed me, not based on my perfection, but His power, not based on my strength, but His Spirit.

Scriptures for the Overcomer

- **Romans 8:37** – *"No, in all these things we are more than conquerors through Him who loved us."*
- **2 Corinthians 12:9** – *"My grace is sufficient for you, for my power is made perfect in weakness."*

AFFIRM

- **Isaiah 41:10** – *"Fear not, for I am with you… I will strengthen you and help you."*
- **Psalm 27:1** – *"The Lord is my light and my salvation—whom shall I fear?"*
- **1 John 5:4** – *"For everyone born of God overcomes the world."*
- **Revelation 12:11** – *"They overcame him by the blood of the Lamb and the word of their testimony…"*
- **John 16:33** – *"In this world you will have trouble. But take heart! I have overcome the world."*

What Do You Do When Fear Tries to Return?

Because it will try, fear doesn't always disappear. It just changes its disguise. So, what do you do when the lies show up again? When the pressure rises? When your chest tightens and your mind starts racing? You stand. But not in your strength. Not in your power. Not in your ability to "push through." You stand by training yourself in truth, found in God's Word. You remind yourself daily of God's words in scriptures such as 2 Timothy 1:7, *"For God has not given us a spirit of fear, but of power, love, and a sound mind."* You remind yourself that God is loving. That God is kind. That God is faithful, even when fear screams otherwise. You anchor your thoughts in the Word as portrayed in Philippians 4:8, *"Whatever is true, whatever is honorable, whatever is right, whatever is pure, whatever is lovely, whatever is admirable, if anything is excellent or praiseworthy, think about such things."* What did God say? That's what you stand on. Not what fear whispers. Not what your emotions shout. But what the Lord declared. I now know that overcoming is not the absence of battle; it's the refusal to back down.

Chapter 3

When God Speaks,

Theme: False narratives, people-pleasing, conformity, and the power of God's affirmation.

Scripture: *"Before I formed you in the womb, I knew you; before you were born, I set you apart; I appointed you as a prophet to the nations."* – Jeremiah 1:5

"Do not conform to the pattern of this world but be transformed by renewing your mind." – Romans 12:2

Prayer: Lord, I thank You for Your whisper—soft, but sure. I thank You for speaking truth over every lie I've believed. Today, I release the need for human approval and embrace the affirmation that only comes from You. Help me to walk boldly in who

When God Stamps His Approval

You say I am, not who the world says I should be. Let my mind be renewed, my confidence restored, and my obedience aligned with Your will. In Your strength, I will rise. In Your voice, I will trust. In Your affirmation, I will move. Amen.

AFFIRM

Blinded

This chapter explores how fear not only binds but also distorts. Fear feeds false narratives that we walk in daily narratives formed by past trauma, societal expectations, and the desire to be accepted by people who were never meant to validate us. But when God speaks, everything changes. His whisper cuts through the noise. His Word affirms what the world never could. The challenge is learning to listen and stand in what He has declared.

You've been conformed, silenced, and molded by false expectations, but now God is calling you to pivot. This is your call to unlearn the lies, quiet the noise, and align with His truth about who you are. You've been approved. You've been affirmed. You've been chosen.

How often have we walked into false narrative stories shaped by fear, rejection, and the opinions of people who were never meant to define us? How many times have we allowed fear and conformity to rob us of the freedom God already gave? Even after hearing God's voice, receiving His promises, and being reminded of His Word, fear still whispered, *"You're not enough."* But what happens when God whispers louder? What happens when He speaks life, purpose, and truth?

God's whisper changes *everything*. It doesn't always come with noise or crowds—it's that still, small voice that says: *"I called you on purpose, for a purpose."* Before you were ever formed, you were already chosen, affirmed, and approved. But the problem is, we don't always *believe* Him. We seek affirmation from people who don't even know our assignment, and we become stagnant chasing acceptance instead of obedience.

God never said everyone would affirm you. He never promised universal acceptance. But He did affirm you Himself. And that changes the trajectory of your life.

The Pivot

When God speaks, He gives you permission to pivot, to move differently, talk differently, and show up differently. To unlearn the lies and live in the liberty of truth. You no longer conform to being seen or celebrated by others. You live to please the One who formed you.
It's not enough to say, *"I'm enough,"* you must *know* it. It's not enough to say, *"I've*

AFFIRM

been approved;" you must *walk* like it. You must live in complete alignment with His affirmation, regardless of who validates you along the way. So, declare this over your life:

- Fear, lies, or the opinions of others do not define me.
- God affirms me.
- I was created on purpose, for a purpose.
- I will not conform, I will transform.
- I stand boldly in God's truth.
- I have everything I need to walk in my calling.
- I am chosen. I am called. I am approved.
- I will no longer whisper doubt; I will declare destiny.
- I am who God says I am.

Chapter 4
From Barren to Fruitful

Theme: From Barren to Fruitful: The Beauty of God's Timing and Truth

Scripture: *"I am the vine; you are the branches. If you remain in me and I in you, you will bear much fruit; apart from me, you can do nothing."* – John 15:5 (NIV)

"Before I formed you in the womb, I knew you; before you were born, I set you apart; I appointed you as a prophet to the nations." – Jeremiah 1:5 (NIV)

"Sing, barren woman, you who never bore a child; burst into song, shout for joy... because more are the children of the desolate woman than of her who has a husband," says the Lord." – Isaiah 54:1 (NIV)

AFFIRM

"Let us not become weary in doing good, for at the proper time we will reap a harvest if we do not give up." – Galatians 6:9 (NIV)

"And we know that in all things God works for the good of those who love him, who have been called according to his purpose." – Romans 8:28 (NIV)

Prayer: I decree and declare over my life what God has spoken and affirmed to me. God said I am the head and not the tail. He said I am above and not beneath. He said I am the lender and not the borrower. He said I can do all things through Christ who strengthens me. It is in His Name that I pray. Amen.

When God Stamps His Approval

Never Give Up. Never Give In.

Oh, what a joyous day when you realize God loves you! He chooses you. And that alone is enough.

But life doesn't always look the way you thought it would.

I've spoken about life. I've pivoted. I've declared the promises of God over myself. And yet… I am barren. I don't have children. At this age, I thought I would. I thought I'd be a mother by now. I thought my life would look a certain way. I didn't expect to struggle with fertility. I didn't expect to feel the ache of unanswered prayers in such a personal, deeply painful way.

Statistics say that many women face fertility issues. Some, like me, have conceived and then lost. I experienced the heartbreak of a miscarriage, and then never conceived again.

This journey has not been for the faint of heart. And yet, through it all, God still loves me.

I remember a specific moment. My husband and I were on a short vacation, a little getaway. I found myself up one morning,

AFFIRM

talking to the Lord in stillness. And in that quiet moment, God said something I will never forget, "Embrace the place you are in."

Embrace this season. Embrace this time of your life. Embrace not having children, right now.

That word was spoken to me about five years ago. And here I am, five years later, still childless, while everyone around me is having children, even their second and third. I celebrate them. Genuinely. I smile. I support. But when I'm alone, I still ask: "God, when is it my time?"

I've read the scriptures. "Children are a heritage from the Lord, and the fruit of the womb is His reward." I've prayed. I've fasted. I've waited. I've believed. But here's what I had to learn:
You can't control everything.
- You can't make yourself pregnant.
- You can't force what hasn't been destined for you yet.
- You can't make it happen; only God can.

Yet... I'm still affirmed. Even in my barrenness, I am affirmed. God whispered to me, "*I created you. I gave you a purpose. I ordained you to go forth.*"

Even though I don't have children right now, I still have His promises, His declaration. I am not defined by my ability to bear children; I am defined by what God says about me.

So yes, I don't have kids at this age, but I still believe in the Lord's report. That belief alone affirms, grounds, and gives me the strength to face another day with purpose. I had to learn to be okay with not being okay. I must sit with the ache and still trust God. I must accept the discomfort of the unknown and still know I'm loved. I must understand that just because it hasn't happened doesn't mean I am forgotten, nor will it ever happen. All things are in God's timing.

One day, I heard the Lord say, "*I'm taking you from barren to fruitful.*" At first, I was excited. I thought it meant I'd have children right away. But God showed me another meaning; He took me in the Spirit from barrenness to fruitfulness.

Not a child in my womb, but fruit from my life. Fruit from my obedience. Fruit from my calling. Fruit from what He birthed inside of me. John 15 rang loudly in my spirit, which

AFFIRM

says, *"Abide in Me and you will bear much fruit."* Stay connected to the Vine. Stay connected to the Source.

This is not about what the world says is fruitful. It's about what Heaven sees as fruitful. Sometimes life doesn't give you the hand you expect. But God always provides you with what you need, even when you doubt, when you're weary, and when the road looks uncertain.

His Word is sure. His promise is eternal. We will reap—if we faint not.

Chapter 5
Approved by God—Now What?

Theme: Walking Boldly in Divine Affirmation

Scripture: *"Oh, that my people would listen to me! Oh, that Israel would follow me, walking in my paths! How quickly I would then subdue their enemies! How soon my hands would be upon their foes!"* – Psalm 81:13-16 (NLT) (This echoes your moment with Psalm 48, where God reveals what could have been if we had obeyed.)

"Be still, and know that I am God." – Psalm 46:10 (KJV)

"Ye have compassed this mountain long enough: turn you northward." – Deuteronomy 2:3 (KJV)

AFFIRM

"Whether you turn to the right or to the left, your ears will hear a voice behind you, saying, 'This is the way; walk in it.'" – Isaiah 27:21 (NIV)

"For God has not given us a spirit of fear, but of power and of love and of a sound mind." – 2 Timothy 1:7 (NKJV)

Prayer: God, I Hear You Now. Thank You for Your voice, for Your affirmation, and for never giving up on me—even when I stood still out of fear, confusion, or pain. Today, I break out of the box I put myself in. I release the need to have it all figured out and instead trust in Your perfect will. I receive Your divine stamp of approval, not as something to sit on, but something to stand in.

Teach me to discern Your voice, not just in the loud moments, but in the still ones too. Help me to know that being still does not mean being stuck. God, ignite the fire in me again to go. Let me go with boldness. Go with courage. Go with confidence.

Lord, if I have circled this mountain too long, show me the way forward. Order my steps. Confirm my direction. And remind me daily that Your yes is enough.

When God Stamps His Approval

I decree that I am no longer bound by shadows, trauma, or doubt. I am affirmed. I am approved. And I am moving forward in Jesus' name. Amen.

AFFIRM

Approved by God—Now What?

There's something sincerely humbling about realizing that God has already given you His stamp of approval. Not because you don't believe in Him, but because you haven't fully believed in yourself. I know that feeling. I've lived it. I remember waking up one morning with the words from a song by Tamala Mann echoing in my spirit: *"While You're Going Through, Let Jesus Work on You."* Another part said, "Be still and know He is God."

In that moment, something shifted within me. I realized that being still doesn't mean being boxed in. It doesn't mean afraid, passive, or silent. It means resting in the assurance that God is in control. His timing is perfect so that His word will not return void. But even as I understood that I had to admit I had still boxed myself in. I had lived with a fixed mindset for far too long. I convinced myself I needed more clarity, confirmation, and "signs." And in doing so, I ignored the simple truth, God had already affirmed me.

He had already said go. He had already said to move. But fear whispered, *"Wait until you're sure."* Doubt said, *"What if you get it wrong?"* Insecurity said, *"Who do you think you are?"* And trauma… trauma screamed, *"You've failed before! Why try again?"*

One morning, while talking to God, He led me to a scripture, Psalm 48:18. *"If only you had paid attention to my commands, your peace would have been like a river, your well-being like the waves of the sea."* That word pierced me. Because I had been telling myself I was obedient, faithful, and trusting. And I was. But I didn't move. And obedience without movement is just disobedience dressed in delay.

God told me, *"You could be flowing in My promises right now. You could be walking through open doors. But you stayed put. You didn't move."* Not out of rebellion, but out of fear. And even then, He reminded me: *"I still affirm you. I still approve of you. I still love you."*

That moment changed everything. Because the truth is, many of us confuse God's stillness with our stagnation. We claim to be waiting on God, when in reality, God is waiting on us. He's already spoken. He's already sent confirmation. He's already opened the door. But we stay. We hesitate. We circle the same mountain; emotionally, spiritually, mentally, over and over again.

AFFIRM

And even with His approval, we feel unworthy. We let past trauma cast a shadow over His promises. We let fear dim the light of His affirmation.

But God is not like man. His affirmation is not temporary. His stamp of approval is not conditional. His yes is still yes.

So now that you know you're approved, I have to ask you: *"What will you do with it? Will you keep waiting for another sign? Will you continue living in the shadow of who you were?"* Or will you show up boldly, knowing that the God of all creation has called, affirmed, and sent you?

Because that's what I had to do. I had to stop living like I was still waiting for God's yes and start walking like I was already sent. And the beautiful part? Even in my delay, He still covered me. Even in my hesitation, He still had a plan. Even in my unfaithfulness to move, He was still faithful to love. So here I am approved, affirmed, and finally moving. Now that I've pivoted, I'm bearing fruit, and I've overcome… I ask myself, what's next? And the answer is simple: obedience. Obedience to walk in what He has already called me to. Obedience to trust Him, even when I don't see it. Obedience to lead, to

When God Stamps His Approval

teach, to serve—because God has approved me. And beloved, so have you. *"For the Lord will guide you continually, and satisfy your soul in drought, and strengthen your bones; you shall be like a watered garden, and like a spring of water, whose waters do not fail."* — Isaiah 58:11 (NKJV)

Stamped. Affirmed. Sent. You are not waiting for your approval. He's already given it.

Chapter 6
Breaking the Cycle

Theme: Released to Rise: Embracing the New, Choosing Freedom

Scripture: *"Do not call to mind the former things, or ponder things of the past. Behold, I will do something new, Now it will spring forth; Will you not be aware of it? I will even make a roadway
in the wilderness, Rivers in the desert."* —
Isaiah 43:18–19 (NASB)

Prayer: Lord, thank You for doing a new thing in me. I release the past and choose freedom today. Break every cycle that no longer serves me and guides me onto the path You've prepared. I trust You to make a way, even in the wilderness. In Jesus' name, Amen.

When God Stamps His Approval

When Freedom Becomes a Choice

We say we want something new. But do we want freedom, or do we want the comfort of routine in a prettier disguise? Cycles keep you stuck in rooms God already opened doors out of. Cycles keep you dressed in chains God already broke. Cycles are not just habits—they are spiritual patterns that manifest as *strongholds* when left unchecked.

But God, in His mercy, calls you to rise. This is your chapter of truth. This is the moment you face the mask, pull back the curtain, and say, "No more."

I sat in stillness one day, reflecting on this book and this journey, and it hit me: cycles. The word came like a flood, not just a random thought but a revelation. Cycles have shaped so much of my life. Cycles are more than routine. They are spiritual patterns—revolving doors of comfort, complacency, distractions, and doubt. Cycles keep you in a place longer than you should have stayed. They wear different masks, familiar relationships, hidden insecurities, and repeated mistakes, but all with the same purpose: to delay destiny. I didn't even realize that I had been living in cycles for the longest time.

AFFIRM

- Cycles of disappointment.
- Cycles of self-doubt.
- Cycles of overthinking.
- Cycles of fear masked as wisdom.
- Cycles of moving... but not really going anywhere.

And the worst part? I was doing the same things over and over, expecting different results. I had gotten used to believing lies about myself. I'd gotten comfortable carrying pain I had long outgrown. And yet, God was speaking the whole time.

He had affirmed me. He had approved me. He had already made a way.

But I couldn't move forward because the cycles were louder than His voice. Recognizing the Pattern. As mentioned in Chapter 5, there was a morning I'll never forget. I woke up to a song in my spirit, Tamala Mann's *"Potter; While You're Going Through, Let Jesus Work on You."* The lyrics shifted into that powerful reminder: *"Be still and know that He is God."* And I thought— being still doesn't mean being stuck. Being still doesn't mean I should stay boxed in or bound. Being still means resting in the *assurance* that God is in control, that He's already spoken, and that He's already moved. The problem wasn't that I wasn't hearing God. The problem was, I didn't believe what He had spoken over me.

He had stamped His approval on me. He had told me the door was open. He had affirmed the calling. But I stayed still in fear, not faith.

God's Word vs. Cycles

One day during prayer, God led me to a passage in Psalms, *"If only you had listened to Me, your peace would have been like a river."* (Psalm 81:13-14, paraphrased). And it broke me. I thought I was obeying, I thought I was moving in faith. But really, I was afraid—afraid to mess up, afraid to go without clear evidence, afraid to fail. And God spoke to me saying, *"I had affirmed you to go. But because you didn't move, you missed the flow."* Let that sink in, God had already spoken, and He had already given approval; but I was still praying for confirmation that I already had received and failed to recognize. His approval didn't come in the way I was expecting it, so I missed it completely. Cycles will trick you into thinking you need more time. Cycles will convince you you're not ready. Cycles will

AFFIRM

tell you to wait until you're stronger, healed, perfect, and qualified.

But God says in Colossians 1:12, "*I have already qualified you. You are already enough. You are already free.*"

The Choice to Be Free

You know what makes cycles so dangerous? They don't look evil. Sometimes they feel safe. Sometimes they look like self-care. Sometimes they even look like spiritual waiting. But when waiting turns into wasting, that's not God. That's a cycle. You've got to be willing to do something different.

There was something I loved doing, it wasn't hurting anyone. Just binge-watching a favorite show. But what I didn't realize was, I was distracting myself from hearing God. I was numbing myself from the call. And I was doing it in the name of relaxation. But really? It was disobedience dressed in comfort.

Cycles, Strongholds, and Masks

So, what are the cycles in the life of a believer? They are often strongholds—deep-rooted thoughts and habits that keep us bound. They are revolving doors that look like opportunities but lead back to the same pain. They are masks, ways we hide the truth from others and sometimes even from ourselves. But here's the good news: God breaks cycles. When you choose to rest in His presence and stop trying to fix yourself and allow God to renew you, everything shifts.

Cycles are broken through:
- Intentional time with God
- Prayer that goes beyond routine
- The Word that affirms your identity
- Worship that breaks through fear
- Faith that says yes when everything else says wait

The Truth That Frees You

Cycles will tell you:
- You're not enough.
- You'll always be stuck.
- You've missed your moment.
- God is disappointed.

But the Word of God says:
- *"You are the righteousness of God in Christ Jesus."* – 2 Corinthians 5:21 (NKJV)
- *"You have been redeemed."* – Ephesians 1:7 (NLT)

AFFIRM

- *"You are reconciled to God."* – Romans 5:10 (NKJV)
- *"You walk by faith and not by sight."* – 2 Corinthians 5:7 (NKJV)
- *"You are accepted in the Beloved."* – Ephesians 1:6 (NKJV)

And if God has affirmed you, who can deny you? When you're ready to move, cycles lose their power when you decide, *I will not go back.* Cycles are broken when you decree, *I am free to be.* Not perfect. Not without questions. But free. Free to walk in the promises. Free to trust the process. Free to become everything God spoke.

So, now that He's shown Himself, will you accept yourself? Will you accept that God has affirmed you? Because when God breaks the cycle, you don't return to it. You rise from it.

Chapter 7
Faith That Overrides Fear

Theme: Fearless by Faith: Resting in Perfect Love

Scripture: *"There is no fear in love; but perfect love casts out fear, because fear involves torment. But he who fears has not been made perfect in love."* —1 John 4:18 (NKJV)

Prayer: Lord, Thank You that Your perfect love drives out every fear. Help me to trust You completely, even when I don't understand. Let my faith rise above my fear, and may I rest securely in Your love and promises. In Jesus' name, Amen.

AFFIRM

Humbled by God

Wow. This chapter, even writing it, humbles me. It feels like a key turned inside of me when God whispered, "*Faith that overrides fear.*"

There are moments in life when faith doesn't just coexist with fear—it demolishes it. It steps in, fully clothed in power and truth, and fear has no choice but to leave. Pain disappears. Shame disappears. Self-sabotage disappears. And the promises of God begin to appear.

Faith is the Key

Faith unlocks the door. Faith is the currency of the Kingdom, as my Pastor Allen often teaches, Without faith, it is impossible to please God (Hebrews 11:6). And with faith—truly abiding, unwavering faith—everything changes.

Perfect Love Casts Out Fear

In another chapter, I spoke about perfect love casting out fear. And it led me to a deeper question of, What is perfect love?

When God Stamps His Approval

God began to show me plainly that He is perfect love. Not just what He gives. Not just what He shows. He IS love. So, if God is perfect love, and perfect love casts out fear, then walking in the fullness of God—resting in His love, His character, His promises—leaves no room for fear to stay.

Think about it, how can fear stand in the same place as the Almighty God? It can't and it won't.

Faith That Demolishes Fear

One morning, God shifted the words in my spirit. Not just "faith that overrides," but "faith that demolishes fear."

Demolishes. Tears it down and destroys it. Leaving no evidence that fear ever lived there. When you truly have faith in God—relying on Him, seeking Him, believing He is who He says He is—fear cannot abide because faith becomes bigger. Faith becomes louder. Faith becomes the foundation you stand on when everything else feels like it's crumbling.

Faith says:
- God is with me.
- God is for me.

AFFIRM

- God will never leave me nor forsake me.
- God knows the number of hairs on my head.
- God holds every one of my days in His hands.

Faith doesn't deny what you see—it just believes more deeply in the One who cannot fail.

When Faith Steps In

It's powerful when you realize faith has stepped in and has taken its rightful place in your life.
- You can't fake faith.
- You can't manufacture faith.
- You either believe or you don't.

Faith will tell you where you really stand. And here's the truth, when faith is alive in you it moves mountains. It stirs you to action. It gives you peace in the storm. It holds you when nothing else makes sense.

I sit and think about the affirmations I've spoken over myself—the words posted above my head, declared in my quiet moments—and it was all to build faith. Because faith doesn't come by feeling. We learn in Romans

10:17 that faith comes by hearing, and hearing by the Word of God.

Faith is Greater Than Fear

When fear says: *You're alone,* Faith says: "*God is Emmanuel—God with us.*" – Matthew 1:23 (NKJV)

When fear says: *You're going to fail,* Faith says: "Greater is He that is in me than he that is in the world." – 1 John 4:4 (NKJV)

When fear says: *It's too late,* Faith says: "*He makes all things beautiful in His time.*" – Ecclesiastes 3:11 (NIV)

Fear and faith cannot occupy the same space. And when you let faith arise, fear must flee.

Letting Faith Abide

The invitation today is simple:
- Let your faith be bigger.
- Bigger than the fear.
- Bigger than the unknown.
- Bigger than the disappointments.
- Bigger than the doubt.

AFFIRM

When God affirms you, when He reminds you of His love and His presence, He's calling you to rest. To believe. To move in confidence.

You don't have to know everything—you just have to know He's with you. You don't have to have it all figured out—you just have to trust His hand. Because when faith overrides fear, you walk in the full assurance that God is God—and He is for you.

Final Thoughts

Faith will move you and say:
- Move.
- Trust.
- Obey.
- Believe

Faith says:
- You are the righteousness of God in Christ Jesus.
- You have the mind of Christ.
- You are more than a conqueror through Him who loves you.

Faith says: "I have Christ in me, the hope of glory."

When God Stamps His Approval

Faith doesn't just override fear—it demolishes it. And that kind of faith changes everything.

Chapter 8

Change in Order to Become

Theme: Transformed to Become: Renewing the Mind for Purpose

Scripture: *"Do not conform to the pattern of this world, but be transformed by the renewing of your mind. Then you will be able to test and approve what God's will is—His good, pleasing, and perfect will."*—Romans 12:2 (NIV)

Prayer: Father God, Thank You for the power to be transformed through the renewing of my mind. Help me release old patterns and embrace the change required to become who You've called me to be. Align my thoughts with Your truth and guide me into Your perfect will. In Jesus' name, Amen.

When God Stamps His Approval

Changed to Become

Oh my God, this is so good to me. Change in order to become. Change—even just the word—often brings a feeling of fear. We shy away from it. We resist it. We run from it.

Because with change comes the unknown. And many of us would rather stay in the discomfort we know than step into a change that feels foreign.

My Personal Struggle With Change

I remember when God first gave me the word change over my life. I didn't want to receive it.

I didn't want to hear it. I fought it. I ran from it. I was afraid of what it would cost me. Because change, by its very nature, means something has to move, something has to be surrendered, and often, something has to be lost.

But here's what God showed me. He shared that change is inevitable. It's a part of life. It's part of growth. It's necessary for becoming everything He has spoken over us.

AFFIRM

Change Is the Doorway to Becoming

One morning, God whispered something that struck my soul, He said, *"Change in order to become."* We say we want to be:
- A successful entrepreneur
- A devoted mother or father
- A faithful daughter or son
- A loving spouse
- A trusted person
- A loyal friend...

We say we want to become these things but becoming demands changing. There are things inside of us that must be transformed:
- Mindsets that must shift
- Habits that must die
- Beliefs that must be uprooted
- Wounds that must be healed
- Heart conditions that must be surrendered

If we don't allow these transformations to take place, then we will stay stuck. We will stay stuck in cycles, trapped in familiarity, unable to walk fully in the affirmation of who God created us to be.

When God Stamps His Approval

The Comfort of the Uncomfortable

We get so used to being uncomfortable that true comfort—real, God-given peace—almost feels strange. We cling to old cycles, old habits, old thinking because they feel familiar. But God is calling us to more. He's calling us to move. He's calling us to change. Calling us to change our thoughts. To change our heart. To change our posture. To change our response. God wants to come in and make, mold, and shape us into the very image of Christ that He desires for us to be. In Genesis 1:26 He has a master plan of creating us in His image, it reads as thus, "*And God said, Let us make man in our image, after our likeness:...*" The mold was created, but through our own insecurities we have warped the mold, and we need to be remolded back into His image. But this transformation starts with our willingness to say, "*Lord, change me.*"

Trusting God With the Unknown

When God spoke "change" over my life, I immediately wanted to ask, *"But what does that mean? What exactly will change?"*

AFFIRM

But here's the truth, we don't have to know. We don't have to have all the answers. We just have to trust the One who holds the answers.

He never said it would be easy. But He did say:
- "*My grace is sufficient for you.*" – 2 Corinthians 12:9 (NKJV)
- "*I will never leave you nor forsake you.*" – Hebrews 13:5 (NKJV)

When change feels terrifying, we cry out to the Father, *"Abba, help me! "Help me change."* There's a song by Tamela Mann that echoes this cry titled *Change Me* and the lyrics are, "*Change me, O God, and make me more like You.*"

If we don't allow God to change us, how can we ever become like Him? I don't know about you, but I'm tired of being stuck because of my own limited thinking. Tired of holding onto the old me. Tired of missing the new thing God wants to do because I'm afraid to let go. It's time to arise. It's time to move forward. It's time to allow God to create in us a clean heart and renew a right spirit within us (Psalm 51:10).

When God Stamps His Approval

Change Is Transformation

When we talk about change, we're talking about transformation. Change, according to the dictionary means, *"To make or become different."* But biblically, it goes even deeper, change is transformation. It is the very act of becoming new—no longer conformed to the ways of this world, but transformed by the renewing of our minds. Romans 12:1-2 reminds us to, *"Present your bodies as a living sacrifice, holy and acceptable to God, which is your reasonable service. And do not be conformed to this world, but be transformed by the renewing of your mind."*

Transformation starts in the mind. It starts with our thoughts. It begins when we say, *"Lord, I surrender—change me."*

An Invitation to Change

Today, God is inviting you:
- Will you allow Me to change you?
- Will you trust Me enough to surrender the old so I can birth the new?

Change is Inevitable

Becoming who you were created to be—is a choice.

AFFIRM

- You have been affirmed by God.
- You have been called for purpose.
- You have been chosen for greatness.

Are you willing?
- It requires change.
- It requires transformation.
- It requires surrender.

Chapter 9
When Enough Is Enough

Theme: Drawing the Line: Choosing Boundaries, Choosing Freedom

Scripture: *"The Lord will fight for you; you need only to be still."* – Exodus 14:14 (NIV)

Prayer: Lord, Thank You for reminding me that I don't have to keep fighting battles You've already won. Help me to know when to stand firm, when to let go, and when to say, "Enough is enough." Strengthen me to choose peace, purpose, and the boundaries You've called me to walk in. In Jesus' name, Amen.

AFFIRM

When I Really Mean Enough is Enough

It's something how often we say, *"I've had enough. I'm tired. I'm frustrated."* But there comes a moment—a real moment—when enough is enough. Throughout this book, my life, and this journey, I've reached places where I've had to say it, not just with my mouth, but with my soul: *Enough is enough.*

I've shared how fear once crippled me, how I allowed the enemy to rent space in my mind. I've talked about the cycles I had to break and the pivots I had to make. But there's a difference between talking about it and deciding to live differently. When you truly know that enough is enough, your life changes. Your vision increases and you begin to see in a different way, for example:
- You start to see life for what it is—a gift.
- You start to accept what God has for you without apology.
- You start to move, because you realize you've been destined for more.
- When you say, Enough is Enough, what exactly are you saying? Enough of what?
- Enough doubting yourself.
- Enough second-guessing the Word God spoke over your life.

When God Stamps His Approval

- Enough trying to please everyone.
- Enough shrinking back.
- Enough self-sabotage.
- Enough hiding behind fear.
- Enough not taking your rightful place.
- Enough staying silent when you have a voice worth hearing.
- Enough delaying your purpose.

You realize *I am enough.* Then you start seeing that word 'enough' in a different light. You begin to speak life and not death. You realize you have spent enough time underestimating the power that God has placed within you. You begin walking in authority and begin speaking affirmations over your life, such as:
- Today, I'm becoming.
- Today, I'm walking in the becoming.
- Today, I declare over my life: Enough is enough.
- What has God said about you?
- That you are chosen
- That you are forgiven
- That you are loved
- That you are created for purpose far greater than you can imagine
- That you can do all things through Christ who strengthens you

AFFIRM

You make up your mind that no longer will I put myself last. No longer will I keep laying down on my dreams, my calling, my destiny. Realizing that today is a new day—a new beginning.

I ask you to examine your life and in a heartfelt gesture to truly ask God, *"God, what does it look like to move your way? To trust your plan fully?"*

Know that God affirmed you before the world began. As Jeremiah 1:5 reminds us: *"Before I formed you in the womb I knew you, before you were born I set you apart."* Move toward your destiny knowing that you were predestined for this. You were chosen for this. You were stamped with God's approval—and no devil in hell can revoke it.

When God speaks a thing over your life, just like He said in Genesis, *"Let there be light,"* and there was light—His Word manifests. It *will* come to pass.

I think about this journey toward my doctoral degree—a seed God planted years ago. It didn't happen overnight. It didn't come without challenges. But when God affirms you, when you're in alignment, even when the days are hard, you can rest assured: He's got you.

Are You ready? Enough is enough means surrendering. Enough of trying to control it all.

Enough of doing it your way. Enough of doubting God's promises.

Confess this over your life today, I surrender:
- My thoughts.
- My plans.
- My timeline.
- My understanding.
- I surrender to His will and His way.

And in that surrender
- I find peace.
- I find rest.
- I find strength.
- I find my becoming.

Because *enough is enough* isn't quitting—it's trusting. It's not giving up—it's giving in to the hands of the One who authored your faith and who promises to finish what He started. In Psalm 46:10 the Psalmist gives a word of advice, "*Be still and know that He is God.*"

AFFIRM

Are you being still? Do you trust Him to be the God of your life?

Enough is enough, resist the devil and he will flee and then know that because I know that I can walk forward, confident, affirmed, and becoming everything God has called me to be.

Chapter 10
Now That You Know

Theme: Walk in Wisdom: Living What You've Learned

Scripture: *"Teach me thy way, O Lord, and lead me in a plain path..."* – Psalm 27:11 (KJV)

"I will instruct you and teach you in the way you should go; I will counsel you with my loving eye on you." – Psalm 32:8 (NIV)

Prayer: Lord, teach me to know the way You would have me to go and the plain path You would have me to take. For Your ways are higher than mine, and Your thoughts higher than mine. Help me to be the light and example You've called me to be. As I shift and transition from place to place in life, help me never to forget that You have affirmed me.

AFFIRM

You knew me before I was born, called me, and predestined me for such a time as this. I stand on Your Word in Psalm 32:8, knowing that You will instruct, teach, and counsel me with Your eyes upon me. Thank You, God, for the transformation. Thank you for the affirmation. Help me to live a life that reflects You in all I do. In Jesus' name, Amen.

When God Stamps His Approval

No Longer Familiar

There comes a time in your life when you look around and realize that the places you used to go, the things you used to do, the fears you used to carry—you don't anymore. Change has taken place. Not just outwardly, but inwardly. You've been affirmed by God.

But let me make this clear—being affirmed doesn't mean the journey of growth is over. Being affirmed is simply the divine confirmation that your life has purpose. That you've been chosen. That the work within you is God-ordained. That He has spoken over your life. And now? Now, it's time to rise.

I remember years ago when I was just beginning to receive and accept the call on my life. I had a dream that I'll never forget. In it, I stood before a judge. He looked at me and said, "Everything you need is in this bag." Then he handed it to me. Before I turned to leave, he added, "I've placed women along your journey—just in case you need help. But know this, I've already given you everything you need."

That dream wasn't just symbolic—it was a prophetic word from God. It was a reminder

AFFIRM

that what I needed was already within me. And friend, the same is true for you. God has equipped you with everything you need—not just for a season, not just for a moment, but for a lifetime. The same God who formed you, who breathed life into you, also placed gifts, callings, and purpose inside of you.

In the early chapters of this book, I spoke about fear—how it sits heavy, how it tries to paralyze. But now that you know you've been affirmed by God, it's time to stand up. Dust off the lies, the labels, the cages you've lived in. It's time to make a declaration over your life.

Declare this with me:
- I am everything God says I am.
- I am bold.
- I am unique.
- I am purposeful.
- I am driven.
- I am called.
- I am loved.
- I am inspired, and I inspire others.
- I am empowered to empower others.
- I can do all things through Christ who strengthens me.
- Nothing can separate me from my purpose or the love of God.

- Greater is He that is in me than he that is in the world.

Saying It Is One Thing, Living Is Another

Living means choosing not to walk as a victim of your circumstances. It means releasing torment, trauma, and the false narratives that have held you back. It means rising above fear, above shame, above doubt—and into purpose.

After God has affirmed you and stamped His approval on your life, the next step is not just acknowledgment, but belief. Do you believe what He's said about you?

In Isaiah 53:1, the Word says, *"Whose report will you believe?"* Will you continue to believe the lies you've told yourself? Will you believe the labels others have placed on you? Will you believe the whispers of the enemy that try to drown out God's voice? Or will you finally believe the report of the Lord?

I know what it's like not to believe. I know what it's like to feel unworthy, unseen, and unsure. I know what it feels like to show up for everyone else while silently questioning

AFFIRM

if you're enough for the assignment God has given you.

But I also know that my Bible tells me in Philippians 1:6, "...*that he which hath begun a good work in you will perform it until the day of Jesus Christ.*"

So today, I challenge you to heal.
- Heal from what hurt you.
- Heal from what haunted you.
- Heal from what hindered you.

Ask God to saturate your soul.
- To rebuild what life has torn down.
- To restore what you've given up on.
- To reveal what's been buried by pain or fear.

This book, this journey—it's not the end. It's the beginning. The beginning of you seeing yourself the way God sees you. The beginning of your walking in boldness. The beginning of becoming everything He affirmed you to be.

I pray you take inventory of your life, not to feel guilt or shame, but to remember how far God has brought you. To remember the divine potential that still lives in you. He has given you the tools. He's provided the wisdom. He's placed destiny inside of you.

So, I ask you this, "How bad do you want it?" Are you willing to put in the work? It's alright to cry when needed? Remember to worship when it's hard? Stand on His word and learn to believe when it doesn't make sense? God has already affirmed you.

Seek Him and begin to ask Him questions, such as:
- Lord, make me become what You have already spoken.
- Make me become the vessel you saw before I was formed in my mother's womb.

Conclusion

The Becoming Continues

As you close this book, I hope you don't close the journey. Everything you've read, reflected on, and felt is only the beginning. This was never just about words on a page; it was about an awakening within. About remembering and about becoming. You have been affirmed, not by people or titles, but by God Himself. You have been called, chosen, and equipped. Now it's time to walk in it.

There may still be battles, still be questions, still be days when you forget who you are—but never forget Who sent you. Never forget that your purpose was never meant to be quiet. It was meant to rise. So, keep rising. Keep healing. Keep becoming. Just know that the world is waiting for the full expression of you and heaven has already said, "Yes."

When God Stamps His Approval

Closing Prayer

Father God,

Thank You for walking with me and with every reader through this journey of becoming. Thank you for the truth you've revealed, the healing you've begun, and the purpose you've affirmed.

Lord, we lay down every fear, every doubt, and every weight that once held us back. We choose to walk in the truth of who You say we are chosen, called, equipped, and empowered.

Help us to remember that You've already affirmed us, already approved us, and already gone before us. Let every step we take be guided by Your Spirit. Let our lives reflect Your glory, and let our hearts remain open to Your continued shaping.

We ask You to renew our minds, strengthen our spirits, and teach us to walk boldly into the purpose You have designed for us. May we never forget that our becoming is a daily journey with You and that with You, we lack nothing.

AFFIRM

Seal this book in the hearts of every reader. Let it stir up purpose, ignite healing, and inspire transformation.

In Jesus' name, Amen.

www.ingramcontent.com/pod-product-compliance
Lightning Source LLC
Chambersburg PA
CBHW060031180426
43196CB00044B/2466